Shoe-ology

from the shamelessly sensible to the wickedly pointed

Karn Knutson

CONARI PRESS

First published in 2006 by Conari Press,
an imprint of Red Wheel/Weiser, LLC
York Beach, ME
With offices at:
368 Congress Street
Boston, MA 02210
www.redwheelweiser.com

Library of Congress Cataloging-in-Publication Data
Knutson, Karn.
  Shoe-ology : from the shamelessly sensible to the wickedly pointed / Karn Knutson.
    p. cm.
  ISBN 1-57324-273-X
 1. Shoes—Humor. I. Title.

  PN6231.S5465K58 2006
  818'.602—dc22

                              2005030289

Typeset in Agenda and Wendy by Kathleen Wilson Fivel

Printed in Malaysia

JP Printers

13 12 11 10 09 08 07 06
  8 7 6 5 4 3 2 1

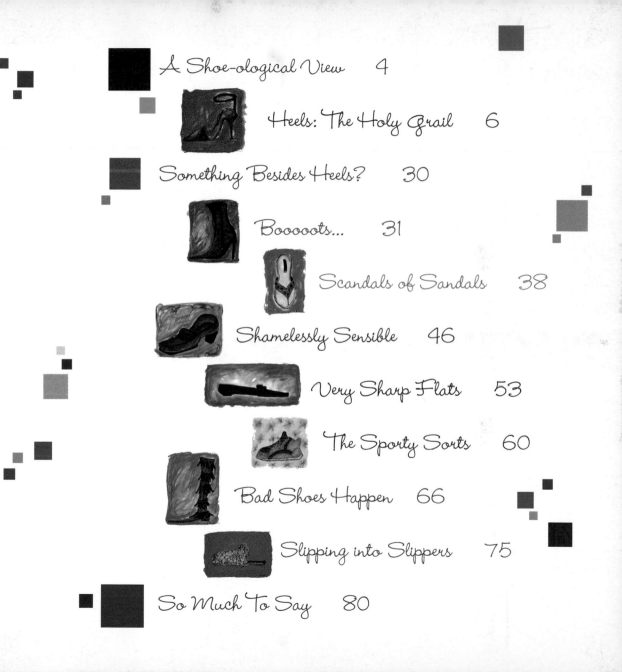

A Shoe-ological View

What are your shoes saying about you?

There is an -ology to explain nearly everything we humans do. From what we think, to why we drink, to our grooming habits before we had salons. Each useful and I'm sure educational, but possibly the greatest of all the -ologies is shoe-ology. The very fashionable examination of who we are by what we wear on our feet. Or to look at it another way, shoe-ology is how to judge a girl by her shoes. (Not that we would ever judge.)

Oh, how far shoes have come from the days of simply offering protection from pebbles and hot sand. You'd think there would be a simple logic to shoes, but no. If you've ever overheard, or been responsible for, the high-pitched squeals emanating from a shoe store, you know shoes and logic don't live in the same hemisphere of the brain. We don't always make the most sense with our footwear choices, but in the sublime arena of shoes, it doesn't matter how twisted or illogical your reasons. As long as they're cute—even if it's only in your eyes.

We lust after them, spend ridiculous amounts to have them, pamper them more than our pets and, in some cases, we might even love them a little more than our boyfriends.

There are shoes that add ten years to your age and pairs that take twice as many points off your IQ. From the moment you slip, strap, or wedge them on, they're telling the world who you are. At least for today, anyway. Sometimes they're speaking of us highly and sometimes you want to wash your shoes' mouths out with soap. They let anyone who's studied in shoe-ology to determine with a mere glance whether you're a fad follower or a true fashionista.

At last, there is the ultimate guide for all you practicing shoe-ologists. Since you've already hunted them, lusted after them, elbowed your way through a designer sample sale, created a shrine-like closet for them, bragged, gushed and cooed endlessly over them, maybe you should see if you agree with what they have to say. Are you cool? Sexy? Dangerous? Do they tell the world you're a saint or a slut? To be feared or forgotten? Aren't you dying to know?

Heels: The Holy Grail

Some women have two categories for shoes: Heels and "Those *other* things that *other* people wear." A slave to their heels, they refuse to listen to any sane voice that tells them how bad they are for the back. For them, heels make you look good and that's what it's all about. Granted, when you start talking about heels you sound a little like Forrest Gump talking about shrimp. You have your high heels, really high heels, mid heels, low heels, kitten heels, wedge heels, spike heels, chunky heels, even no-heel heels for the flat-phobic and the heel snobs who need to justify why they're on the beach wearing wafer-thin flip-flops with no discernible heel height in sight.

When your heels are talking about you, they start with "Look at me!" and go from there. They can say something as simple as "I like me," to something as complicated as, "I'd like you to like me, but I'm not going to let you know that until you've proven yourself worthy."

The take-away from a well-chosen pair can be sex, confidence, or danger. And when the stars align right, all three at once. There's nothing accidental about sliding into heels, so regardless of whether they are friend or foe, they always have scads to say.

Strappy Red Satin

At the office, this is a dead giveaway—you want to be anywhere but where you are. Preferably with some tall, dark, handsome man or with friends that make you laugh so hard you snort.

You know you're smarter than your boss and so does your boss's boss. When you walk into a meeting with "The Boys," you take full advantage of being able to keep them off balance, straddling the line between attraction and fear.

Wheeeeeeeeee!

Anyone up for fun? We know you are. Wearing something that resembles a roller coaster lets the world know your approach in one glance. "Strap In and Let It Go."

You love the platform wedge, not only for the way it screams, "I'm fabulous!", but for that extra little something it gives your walk. You magically turn any bit of sidewalk into your own private runway show. Work it baby, work it, let your inner rockstar shine.

Equal Opportunity Bling

Not so much a shoe as it is jewelry for your feet. If you could afford them in diamonds, you wouldn't think it the least bit frivolous.

Your jewelry box overflows, covering your dresser. There are dangly, shiny piles of things scattered all over your house. Every body part that can support something, does. Ears, ankles, wrist, neck, bellybutton, waist, even the toes, so why not your feet? Because, in the language of accessorizing, you were born fluent.

Beaded Love

Okay, so you don't make the most practical choices, but they make sense to you. The restaurant you choose is determined by the distance you'll need to walk to get there. After all, these cherished beauties are hand-beaded, hand-cut crystal over Italian silk. You'd happily spend more on the cab than dinner to avoid causing damage.

The Closet Stripper

Your "goodie drawer" isn't just next to the bed, it takes up half the closet. Every now and then, you flash a little move that makes your fellow party-goers wonder, "Just how *exactly* did you work your way through graduate school?"

Your significant other loses the ability to form complete sentences when these are on your feet for the evening. Of course, you're not planning on the evening lasting very long.

Color Blinded

If your audience can shake themselves loose from the hypnotic effects of your alternating hues, they will see yours is a simple message.

"I'll buy anything in my favorite colors. Even if I have nothing to go with it. I don't understand people who don't wear color. It hurts my teeth to imagine the sight of their closets, nothing bright, vibrant, or bold in sight. I love color. Especially *my* colors. My colors are my signature."

Two-Toned in Perfect Pitch

It's what you'd expect to see on the foot of a "lady who lunches."
She's coifed from head to toe. The leather detail of her shoes
matches her bag, her nails, the wallet that holds the platinum cards,
and the interior of her two-seater convertible (a little birthday
gift from hubby number three).

Architectural Feet

The shoe itself belongs in a museum and you belong in the hall of fame for keeping it on, which you don't always do. You're clueless that anyone walking with you is moving at a snail's pace to not leave you in the dust. It's one step, two . . . "Oops." Step, step. "Oops." You get there eventually, and with any luck someone called ahead to change the reservation.

The Bow

You use the word *cute* in the most inappropriate places and to you being stylish is being pretty. Being sexy is being pretty. Cool—pretty. Smart—pretty. Pretty much, life is being pretty. Your hair is never severe, it's pretty. Your smile is bright and always present, and you may have been born wearing pearls. You have a sweetness that rivals saccharin, but no one really minds, because you're just so gosh darn pretty.

The Minimal Mule

You know you'll throw a shoe at least once an evening, but you've perfected aiming it at the cutest guy in the room. It's a guaranteed conversation starter and gives you a chance to try out the "Prince Charming, slip-on-my-shoe" routine. That being just one of the hoops your potential suitors will be jumping through. After all, if you're skilled enough to navigate in something so barely there, the boy has to have some skills of his own.

The Pain Inflictor

Their piercing presence instills fear in the hearts of men everywhere. They may have their power ties, but you know what really takes command of a room—a wickedly pointed toe flowing down from an equally sharp heel.

It gives you a little adrenaline rush every time you glance down and see that point jutting forth from beneath your perfectly tailored trouser. Look out world, look out boys!

It's irrelevant that your toes want to file for divorce every time you slide these killers on, because you wouldn't trade them for the world. After all, ruling the world is your goal and these are the shoes you'll be wearing when you conquer it.

"These old things?"

You're the one who shows up looking flawless even in jeans and a T-shirt. You always have the greatest shoes. Fresh off the designer runway, yet you wear them with as little care as last summer's flip flops.

Even your best girlfriends hate you a tiny bit for seeming so perfect and take just a little pleasure when one of your few and minute flaws sneaks to the surface.

You're mostly modest, but deep down, you know you're fabulous.

Are the Bells Ringing?

Here comes the bride. . . and hopefully you're actually getting married. If you are, your wedding day is stunning. You've spent several hours determining which mint cups should be on the tables, not to mention a small fortune on invitations and another on flowers. Your shoe design, like your "I need a tow truck" ring, is flawlessly one-of-a-kind.

However, if you're single and there's no long-awaited ring on your finger, the story is a little different. These shoes are saying you're a hopeless, if not desperate, romantic. You're searching every corner for the rider of a white horse. They signal to any potential knight to run for the hills because you'll be looking for a proposal on date two and two kids in the suburbs by date four.

"OOOOOOOh, so cute!"

You squealed, ran in, grabbed them, and caressed them as if they were your newborn child. Then you proceeded to spend the equivalent of that child's college education for them.

You nearly prance when you have them on. You cross and re-cross your legs in any social setting and tend to drop pencils, forks, and small animals near your feet just to draw a tad more attention to them. You're sure everyone wants to look at your shoes as much as you do and you can't understand how they can do anything else when you're around.

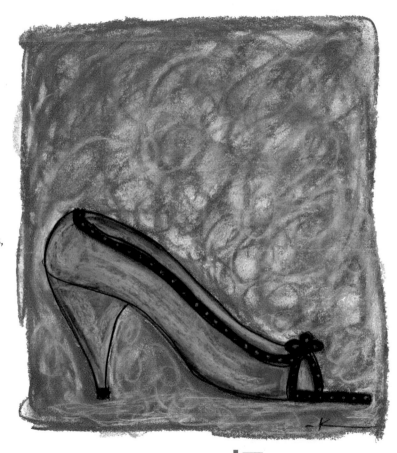

Prim, Proper, and Purring?

Every mother who was a looker in her youth has this shoe. If you're wearing it and are young enough that your mother is still a looker, you're dreaming of having the same cookie-cutter, picture-perfect life you believe your parents have.

You dress a good decade beyond your age. Your thank-you notes, and there are always thank-you notes, are sent the very day you receive the gift, kind gesture, best wishes, or the bag boy remembers to place the eggs on the top of the bag. You think mini-vans are sexy, but will only say the word *sexy* in a giggle-covered whisper.

The best little secret these sensible pumps have to share: still waters run kinky. Try as you might to channel June Cleaver, those who speak "shoe" are taking bets that behind your closed suburban doors you're a wild child between your 600-thread count, matching dust-ruffle sheets.

A classic fur-trimmed mule makes you feel like you're in the boudoir even when perusing the power tools at the hardware store. You somehow manage to have a full face of makeup, even when awoken at 3 a.m. Your clothes have a flowy quality to them as if your occupation is actually lounging. Regardless of your size, you seem to 'flit' from place to place. You call everyone "Honey," from your teacup poodle with its rhinestone collar to the 16-year-old delivery boy, who you shamelessly flirt with until he turns the same shade as your Danger Red lipstick.

The Almighty Mule

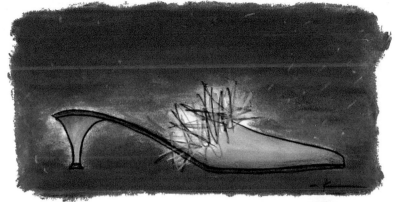

Lingerie of the Feet

Your shoes match your style of dressing. Which is, "As little as I can get away with without being a moving violation." And these skimpy darlings speak for you so well. "I'm trying to not be wearing shoes while wearing shoes that look fabulous and extremely sexy. They're like lingerie for my toes. They cover just enough to keep you guessing and have a skinny little strap to hold them on, but make them very easy to slip off."

Something for a Summer Fling

You have a playful side that you tend to keep in full view. You may not be the most practically dressed for the occasion, but you always look adorable. Even when struggling to keep your heels from sinking into the grass at a garden party, or your toes and lips are turning blue because open-toed shoes and capris may have not been the *best* choice for a moonlit-cruise. You only whimper occasionally through your "Oops, silly me!" smile, as you cozy up to your escort and switch from martinis to hot toddies. Problem solved, or at least forgotten.

Such a Pretty Puzzle

Something about you leaves most people wondering and whispering amongst themselves. Because these aren't your Aunt Millie's Mary Janes.

You may sit with your ankles crossed, sip tea with pinky extended, and act as coy as a geisha, but that's in public . . .

In private, what are your dark secrets? Fetishes, vices, guilty pleasures? You are an enigma and you like it that way. You're the one other women are a little afraid to know and men are a little more afraid to date.

Good and Devilish

This shoe might look like an angel from the back, with a little halo ankle strap, but from every other angle it's all horns and tail and tellingly tight leather. You speak softly and carry a very big sexy stick.

Peek-a-Boo-Hoos

You really want to like your feet, but you don't. This shoe creates the illusion that you're showing something off, nearly being naughty. Fooling the onlookers into believing that you're not horrified to let anyone see your naked little digits. If you weren't afraid of losing a toe, you'd even have your pedicurist wear a blindfold.

Not-so-Secret Weapons

Spikes are a Bond-Girl-in-Training's best friend. A deadly weapon that is guaranteed to distract any adversary and can double as a killer letter opener, so as to avoid chipping a nail opening those top secret cables.

If you're *not* chasing international jewel thieves, you may be ever so slightly addicted to heels. In that case, these are your own personal billboard and the message is clearly spelled out in pink patent leather and steel. "Look out girls, if I'm coming for your man, these are going to leave a mark."

Socialite Risqué

You've taken the idea of a bare midriff in a completely different direction—one that fits in your teeny tiny window of racy behavior.

If there's a gene for the Upper East Side, you have it. Always classy, always classic. Your eternal hairstyle is as well trained as your plaid-clad terriers.

Your throw pillows were placed by your interior designer and have never occupied any other positions. Even your pajamas visit the tailor before they make their way into your alphabetically ordered, custom-built closets.

For you, champagne is the only choice and caviar is a food group (the non-endangered kind, of course). After all, charity causes are your second favorite accessory.

The Crossover

So deceptively simple because you wear them so well. No one would ever know it takes you three tries, each shoe, to get your toes on the right sides of those slinky little straps. It's not that you're being rude when you refuse to take off your shoes to walk across your host's new hardwood floors—not at all. It's vanity, darling. You don't want anyone watching you attempt to reshoe yourself with the same effort involved in solving an astrophysics problem.

Skin It and Make It Beg

There's something sensibly terrifying about you. You're impeccable in your power couture and cynicism is your native tongue.

There is no mistaking, no matter the title on your business card—Lawyer, Editor, Executive VP of whatever—the fine print reads, "I am in charge, or will be soon, and there's nothing you can do about it except sit back, preferably out of my way, and watch the show."

Itty-Bitty-Bondage

Providing more questions than answers with your mischievous grin, you sashay by in these treats of leather and metal. Onlookers might have trouble taking their eyes off your feet long enough to make their way up to your face. You can see the wheels turning as they hold themselves back from asking, "Is this the day wear of a dominatrix?", "Do you have your whips and riding crops arranged by size or degree of pain?", or "Is this as far on the wild side as you're willing to go?" For now, anyway.

Something Besides Heels?

Now for all those *other* things *other* people wear. Yes, contrary to what some women believe, it is possible to wear something besides heels and actually look mighty good doing it.

However, if you're having trouble breathing at the thought of anything lower than a one-inch kitten heel, brace yourself, slip into something strappy, and see how the rest of the world walks. You know—those people who don't take cabs three blocks because they didn't just have to have the four-inch, blue satin criss-cross strap sandal that the store only had in a half-size too small.

Booooooots . . .

Oh, the joy of boots. Like magic, they have the ability to make the male of the species lose their power of speech and elevate your ego to rockstar status.

It's possible to indulge yourself with above-the-ankle, mid-calf, below-the-knee, above-the-knee or mile-high. You're usually going for strong, sexy, and sharp when you slide them on, because there's just something about a boot you can't get from any other shoe.

Maybe it's the reaction they produce from most men. They stare gleefully and mumble "boooots", with little smirks across their faces. Some of the thigh-high varieties have been known to cause spontaneous fans to follow a well-worn pair for blocks beyond their destinations.

Boots inhabit a world all their own and every female worth her "FE-ness" should have the stamp in her passport.

Boot Seasoned

You can't wait for the temperature to drop or the night air to have a chill. You watch the Weather Channel in summer in hopes of a freak cold snap.

You love the sound the zipper makes as it crawls up your calf. To you, these boots are sexier than any teetering toe strap and pencil thin heel, especially since you can actually walk in them. Correction—you can *stride* in them. Confidence is so sexy, especially in a boot.

You'll wear them with anything. If you thought you could pull it off with a bikini, you'd wear a pair to the beach. The only thing holding you back is the threat of a really ridiculous tan line.

The Boot-ette

You never fully commit. You like to keep your options open. You want the height and sexiness of a heel and the toughness of a boot. And you want to be able to switch freely between them, repeatedly, and with no advance warning or apparent reasoning what-so-ever—much the same way you handle your opinions, menu selections, and boyfriends.

Wanna be a cowboy, baby?

You are an urban cowgirl looking for some boots to knock. Your dream man comes with a big belt buckle, a little twang, and denim that looks good in the saddle.

Your jeans are as tight as a second skin and you wear them every way they come. Low-slung, low-rise, brand spankin' new, broken-in, worn-out, every shade of blue, butt-hugging skirts, and oh-so-short shorts. Accompanying them all, any day and especially night, are your favorite little pair of giddy-ups.

Hello Thigh

These boots are made for anything at anytime. No practicality in sight. Polite society may not be ready for you, but that's just too damn bad. You're here and you're staying. Unless of course, the party is boring.

When you're slipping into the limelight, these are your beloved double-take devices. You simply smirk, knowing people are clueless about what to do with you.

Paired with a leg-screaming skirt, these bad boys announce your presence a good two blocks away. Once you've gotten everyone's attention, the high gloss sensations running from thigh to toe tell them you're not afraid of power, you're not afraid of kinky—hell, you're not afraid of much. So if you're the timid kind, approach with caution.

Grrrrrrrrr

You are a sex cat, the jungle kind—no kittens here. Your favorite costume at Halloween is Catwoman. Actually, it's your favorite costume on the occasional Tuesday evening.

Your temper is anything but a purr. Get in your way and it's a front row seat at Wild Kingdom. You want people to know you're not one to be messed with. So you figure, why make them stretch their puny intellect to figure it out? I'll just broadcast it with every catwalk-worthy strut I take.

Militant Girls of the World

These eternal toughies are worn by many. You'll find them on artsy students, punk rockers, prissy girls trying to piss off their parents, and all sorts of angry activist minds. But it takes a closer look to see where the wearer stands.

Tattoo—check. Opinion on all things political—check. If the boots are scuffed, both things are real. If the boots have a buff to match your nails, they were bought with someone else's credit card and your rebellion is slightly lacking in rebel.

If covered in random splashes or hand-painted to be your own front page, your activism comes in the creative form. Your visual expressions are of the deep and meaningful, if not slightly ugly variety.

Do you Ugg® or Ugh?

You're in one of two camps with these furry little friends on your feet.

The first is the outdoorsy, surfer girl who's hanging with the boys, the dogs, the eclectic groups of humans for which there are no categories. You go for pure function. These are warm. They smash into a backpack—no problem, no lacing, easy on and off—and they're like being barefoot without being cold.

There's a hint of eternal sun on your cheeks and your hair has highlights only Mother Nature could be responsible for. You're the girl everyone loves, beautifully low maintenance, and the occasional envy of any girl experiencing momentary high-heel exhaustion.

The second group wants us to think they're the first group. But, no. This is where the Ugg becomes the Ugh. You think you're so cute that you can shuffle around in your slippers on steroids and your low-slung, too-tight sweatpants that have never known sweat, but are just the thing to let everyone else keep tabs on what color thong you're flossing with today. Your hair, nails, and boobs are all fake or trying to be. You speak in a language of pout and eyelash batting that drops a man's IQ and raises a woman's lunch.

Scandals of Sandals

They can't help but make you happy. If for no other reason than it's generally warm when you wear them. But not every sandal devotee agrees with having to consult the weatherman about their shoe choices, unless he's really cute. Let's hope for these ladies that they keep significant others around who don't mind defrosting their toes from time to time.

Pretty Pretty Pedicure Princess

It's all said with a flitty little voice, while taking tiny little steps. "I'm a girly-girl. I like all things shiny and pretty. Sparkly shoes, sparkly toes. See them glitter in the sun. There's nothing that buying something sparkly won't fix, especially a new pair of shoes to show off the shiny new color of my pedicure today. Pretty, pretty, pretty. If I can't be found for a meeting, I'm probably in a foot bath somewhere."

Bedazzled and Bejeweled

Truth be told, these shoes went with an outfit that was in style for about five minutes and were the only good things to come out of your sister's wedding.

You like the tinkly noise the crystals make when you walk or cross your legs. It makes people look—always a good thing. You wear them with all black, which increases their nearly neon quality. Also, it's the only color you can wear them with, you've never found this particular shade of green occurring on anything else that didn't come with a radioactive warning wrapped around it.

Logo Everything

Trust us—we hear you! How could we not? You're a walking ad. "I am a logo addict. I don't care how much it costs, if it has a designer logo on it, I want it. I'll pay as much for a pair of flip flops as a used car. (Of course, I'd never be caught dead in a used car.) As long as the logos are easily seen, I don't care how something fits or looks, which causes some to call me a fashion victim. But have you seen me? Everything I own is designer, how could I ever look bad? I mean, really? A victim?! It's designer!"

Hippy Happiness

At least one article of your clothing is made from hemp and likely one of your recreations too. You smell of patchouli and consult your star chart as to when it's time to cut your hair—which isn't often. You're a vegetarian for all the usual reasons and a few of your own that you only discuss with your pet canary, Yang, who flies freely around your apartment because you don't believe in cages.

You never leave the house in anything that hides your turquoise and silver bellybutton ring handcrafted by a Native American artist you traded with at the last Burning Man. You have found and embraced your inner flower child, even though you were born and raised in beautiful downtown Burbank by conservative suburban-dwelling parents. Peace and love.

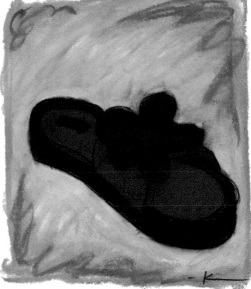

Sand in My Toes

You have a tan at all times on all parts, visible or not. You have far too many bikinis and just as many toe-baring thongs to match. Even your 'real world' clothing has an airiness that cries out for a surf and seagull soundtrack.

You are perpetually on your way to or from some tropical locale, even if it's only the cabana-esque decor of every room in your house. So until your next holiday—somewhere your shoes will spend more time dangling from your fingers than on your feet—the sensation of leather between your toes will have to make do. That, and those little umbrellas in your drinks.

The People's Shoe

Here we have it—any foot, any time of year. Just add socks to get you through a cold winter. Yes, it makes them a fashion ARGH but utility wins here.

Nature made and boringly simple, they keep your feet off the ground and the sex crazed off your trail. When you're wearing these, no one expects you to bother with fashion, make-up, or hair products. Not even a brush. You obviously have the world's issues on your mind, not the latest issue of *Vogue*.

One Little Piggy

"Are those comfortable?" "Does your toe feel claustrophobic?" "They freak me out." "I don't get it." This is the serenade that accompanies your leaving the house, or before if you have roommates. This strange little idea of a shoe goes for minimalism. You bought these, and quite a few other things, after uttering the words, "Cool. Those are different." Not good. Not bad. Just different.

You like things unique, odd, unusual, original, or downright weird. A person should never expect to arrive and leave your house quickly, unless they keep their head down and eyes fixed solely on their own shoes. Because once they begin to look at the kaleidoscope of objects filling all imaginable spaces, they're dumbfounded—much like when they're trying to figure out if you're wearing those shoes because you're mad at your big toe.

Cheap, and Lots of Them

It's not that you're addicted to shoes—you're addicted to being fully coordinated. So you love buying cheap shoes—it lets you have at least one pair for every outfit in your closet. And they *are* outfits. Mix-n-match does not work for you. If you're dressed for sunny weather and it starts to rain before you leave the door, there's no option but to change completely into a rain-appropriate ensemble.

Discomfort doesn't faze you. As long as everything matches, you'll sit and swelter if the outfit just isn't as cute without the sweater. And you'll shiver yourself blue before throwing on a jacket that doesn't compliment your head-to-toe raspberry sherbet color scheme, the shoes for which you spotted in the checkout lane at the local Mega-Mart next to your favorite rag-mag. Both items you bought for less than five bucks.

Shamelessly Sensible

Sensible. It's not a dirty word. Some of the most important decisions in the world are made by minds whose feet reside in sensible shoes. They may not be what you'd don for a hot date, but they're quite perfect for a hot debate. Sensible shoes may be healthy for your feet, but they don't have to make your ego ill. It's all about the attitude within.

Preppy Spoken Here

"I am Ivy League. I've had boyfriends named Biff, Cliff, and Chet. My sport of choice is brunching at the club. I have at least one postgraduate degree, earned because I felt I hadn't devoted enough time to that area during my double major undergrad. When I decide to have children, they will be scheduled—from conception to delivery and all activities from that point forward. My sense of humor is so dry, on the rare occasion I laugh, I become parched. Please pass the imported sparkling mineral water, crystal glass, crushed ice with a twist of lime. Not a slice, a twist."

Let's Go Clogging

Oh, the clog. Sharing a name with something you have to work out of the drain, they have a similar effect on your sex appeal. Onomatopoeically, they're perfect. The clog looks and fits just like it sounds.

You go for comfort and simplicity. It's a safe bet you have tree-hugging tendencies, especially if you're shod in the forest-green, thick wool-felt variety. But you're not expecting anyone to remember you for your footwear—that's what your opinions are for.

Beautifully Worn

You're aware of fashion, you just don't wear fashion. Everything you wear is timeless. As in, you don't remember how long you've had it.

These are the shoes of utility. Walk for miles, work for hours, and step in puddles without thinking, because what you're transporting is more important.

If you can still call them oxfords by what's left of their worn bits, these shoes should receive an honorary Ph.D. for their time of service.

Some form of creative dust covers these shoes, as well as your clothes, your face, and is permanently parked under your fingernails. That, however, is where their certain charm comes from. These are the shoes of the artsy-fartsy. They may not be much to look at, but they are there amidst the musing, while beautiful things are being made.

Shoes and Car to Match

You'd prefer to have a driver than to be one, unless of course, the keys are to something imported and ridiculously fast. You wear your status symbols sublimely, as if unaware that every possession in your possession has a designer pedigree.

These nubby little darlings are the soul saviors of every worldly traveler. Tucked neatly in your to-die-for designer bag, you slip out of your killer heels and into these before you slip aboard the jet. Private, of course.

Nerd Sexy

Oxymoron? Not if you wear them well.

The style says, "I am all business, I can't be bothered with silly straps or teetering heels. I need a shoe that will not pinch my toes as I'm climbing the corporate ladder."

But your choice of the high-gloss, green alligator skin variety tells us slightly more. Particularly when you're sporting them in the front row, in the kind of club where sitting doesn't occur, especially not in the restroom. These let the world know your brain is as big as your mouth and conservative only applies to your clothes.

Sandal Wannabe

This shoe keeps telling itself it's a sandal, and so do you. But really, it's just an open-toed, open-back shoe. Its big square heel gives way too much stability, keeping it from ever escaping being sensible. Something your friends remind you of every time you show up in this ugly stepsister of a sandal. It's like being stuck in coach with a view of first class.

True, the height gives a slight shape to your calf, but the overall blockiness keeps these wannabes from barely registering on the cuteness meter. And we all know a true sandal must invoke, at least to some degree, "Oh, those are cuUute."

Lunch Lady Look

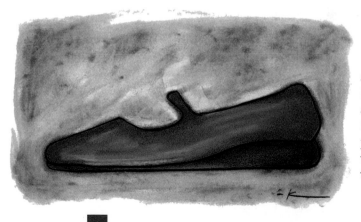

You're telling the world, "Don't look at me," and the world thanks you for it. If you're not tired, you look like you are, at least from the ankle down. And just like the thinnest princess heel can make you feel light as air, these will make you feel and look like you're a potato ready for mashing.

Clownish but Comfy

Your fashion sense has influences from places other than the runways. Since your eighth birthday party, when your mother hired Rompo the clown to entertain, your unspoken obsession has grown—from your penchant for polka-dotted clothing to your college boyfriend with the impossibly curly red hair. As long as you maintain that you love your big, round, red shoes for their spacious fit and aren't still pining for Rompo, your friends will refrain from staging an intervention.

Faithfully Dull

Far from bewitching, these are the shoes found in offices everywhere. They are the loyal companions of the pantsuit, from the smallest cubicle to the snobbiest of boardrooms. This shoe draws so little attention, some people would never guess you're wearing any kind of heel. How could they? They're barely aware you have feet when you're wearing these.

You don't particularly like being *average* height. In your mind, you are statuesque, even if you're only 5'3", and that's when your posture is good. So you found the perfect solution, the shoe version of white noise—always there, serving the purpose of adding three inches, but going mostly unnoticed.

Stand tall, little lady—everyone else thinks you are.

Very Sharp Flats

This is a shoe for anyone with a fear of heights, a fear of their own height, or anyone with a really short boyfriend. These are the women who inhabit the world of flats.

Often mistaken for a subset of sensible, flats are their own animal—a very non-wild, intentionally demure, most often practical, and practically never a risk to an ankle kind of animal. While nearly every woman can manage something sensible, not everyone has the heart for flats.

"I am tall."

"I am very, very tall. Even when I'm seated, you are shadowed by my height. After greeting me, people glance at my feet to see how high my heels are, then they try to keep their eyebrows from raising when they realize there are no heels. It's all me. My shoes are extremely well maintained. They have to be, because no pant leg ever seems to be long enough to provide anything but a modicum of shade."

Shoes as Sole

You don't really think about your shoes. The few you own are non-descript, in both color and style. Any shoe that has the possibility to slip off or twist your ankle is ridiculous in your opinion. You've been known to leave the house having forgotten your shoes and not realizing it until your feet hit something sticky on the street.

That's what you love about these—they're somewhat of a condom for your feet. Easy to slip on, snug fit, don't look like much, but give you traction and protect you from all the icky things you might get into out in the world.

The Phases of Flat

The Full Flat

Perfect for those whose fear of heights is beyond ridiculous. Plus, they prevent restaurants from getting pissy when you try to come in barefoot.

The Demi Flat

For that little extra lift. The same idea as your bra, but in a shoe. They are nowhere near a heel, but they're as high as you can go without getting your boyfriend a booster seat.

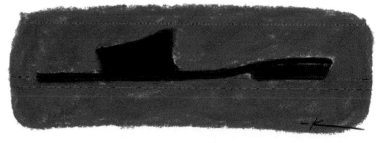

The Trainer Flat

You're toying with the idea of a heel (not in the near future, but someday, before you die) and these are what you start with as you say, "Hi. I'm Jane, and I'm a stiletto-phobic."

Private Garden Party

You spend most of your time socializing with your plants. Since you can't stay in the greenhouse forever and you can't take your garden with you, you love wearing anything that resembles some sort of leafy growing thing. Especially your satin, ivy-green slip-ons with their velvet vines and sequin leaves. You simply love them and don't care if they make you over- and underdressed for every possible occasion. Their soft, nearly-not-there soles keep you close to the earth, making you very happy, because you secretly wish you were something leafy, vining your way up the side of a building, lounging in the sun, being pretty and producing oxygen all day.

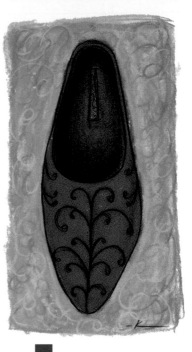

Quiet in the Library

You have a killer collection of eyewear. Your hair is long but no one actually knows because it's forever knotted up on top of your head, secured with a pencil, chopstick, or on rare occasion, an actual item designed for hair. You spend more time in a book than in real life and tend to get the two confused. Your lack of attention during idle conversations is often mistaken for absent-mindedness. Really, there's just too much information rolling around in your head, some of which occasionally spills out. Like when you are asked your shoe size and you respond with a 'brief' history of the craft of cobbling.

Woven Wanderlust

You live in the suburbs and have a pair of these to match every twinset you own. The most excitement you see is when a PTA meeting gets *rowdy* over whether brownies are acceptable for the annual "Cookies-A-Yum-Yum" bake sale.

But these dull wonders let you fit right in with every other mom/wife/homemaker in your two-story, attached garage, picket-fenced and manicured lawn world.

Who knew Prozac® came in economy-sized bottles?

The Sporty Sorts

As long as there have been activities, there have been specific shoes to go with them. Initially intended to enhance performance (but not necessarily looks), shoes of sport have become shoes of fashion and you no longer need to be able to pronounce the name of the sport to sport the shoes. Contrary to logic, athletic and sporty can be mutually exclusive.

Ready, Set, Go Sporty

You seem to be forever coming from the field, the gym, the match, the game, the playoffs, the championship, or the whatever. You are ready to run anywhere, especially if it's after a ball of some sort.

Your entire life is one big gym bag—you stash sports "stuff" under your bed, in every closet, and even in your desk drawers. You've accumulated an impressive array of gear, the bulk of which you have stacked in the hallway or forever jammed in the trunk of your car.

Your shoes are the latest, but not for their style. It's all about the technology—the latest, greatest innovation that lets you run, jump, or dig in better than before.

It takes threats of physical harm for your friends to pry you out of your beloved trainers and into heels. Once the pygmalion transformation is complete, there are at least a few rounds of shots before you attempt to leave the house wearing something that does not have a multi-panel performance sole and impact resistant toe shield.

Oooohhhhhmmmm . . .

You are in touch with your inner self. At least the part of you that signs up for classes at the gym based on what shoes you'll need to be appropriately attired. (If you actually attended.) You might have skipped the class, but you look the part when you meet your friends for a post-workout latte.

As they tell you how invigorating the session was, you assertively state you'll be there next week. Of course you've already forgotten when the class is, because you've just spotted a shoe belonging to an exercise you haven't signed up to not do yet. And it's really cute.

Stuck on the Greens

Your daily life may have nothing to do with scores or chipping wedges, but no one would know it by your shoes. When asked, people usually guess your profession to be a high school gym teacher.

Your poly-cotton knit polo shirt is tucked snugly into your pleated-front khakis. A well-cinched belt keeps them up, although they are really in no danger of falling down. The waistband is so tight, breathing requires conscious thought.

In spite of your vast collection of sun visors, you've developed a permanent squint, making you seem perpetually upset or angry. Then again, it could be that damn waistband restricting your blood flow that's pissing you off.

All Feet on Deck

They may be called boat shoes, but yours, made of Italian calf skin, have more to say than port and starboard. "My wardrobe consists of striped things. I believe 'draped over the shoulders' is the only place to carry your matching sweater. My neck, fingers, and wrist are no stranger to gold. I like things painted white. I like earth tones. Beige, taupe, and tan are distinctively different colors and not at all boring. I have special forks for serving oysters, others for snails, and a pan reserved solely for poaching salmon. I don't throw parties—I entertain. And I believe shoes, when dirty, should be wrapped in tissue and neatly placed in the trash."

The Sport-ette

Even if you're a head-to-toe sports girl, you have to relax once in a while. This shoe looks like it should allow activity, but jogging for the bus is the most distance it will ever see. To you, this is a slipper, a sandal, or a 'girly' dress shoe. It's as far as you'll get from a trainer without someone holding a starter gun to your head. But, not to worry. On you, these work perfectly, because there's nothing in your closet that wasn't designed to "wick away moisture" or layer comfortably under a fleece.

Unfortunately for this clever shoe, it attracts a less authentic wearer. You know who you are, even if you won't admit it. You want to appear athletic, but sweating is icky. You tend to like men who come complete with a six-pack of abs and those men usually like 'active' girls. So you show up for a hike in these and your designer activewear, and no one is surprised when you demand the first aid kit for a broken nail. Unfortunately for you, your distinctive air of poseur only repels the six-pack man, not the mosquitoes.

Bad Shoes Happen

Honestly, there are some pretty frightful things cluttering the world of shoes. Things the other shoes wished were called something else. There are pairs that someone, somewhere thinks are irresistible, but cause most women to look like they've smelled something wretched.

Even still, most shoes have a time and place for which they are ideal. Outside that perfect context, they can be amusing, confusing, or downright dangerous. When we have the misfortune of encountering them, all we can do is try to help the wayward wearers see their footwear errors—and then hide their hideous shoes when they're not looking! Footwear aficionados know the theory of evolution just hasn't caught up to these 'shoes' yet.

"Bless her heart . . ."

It's what they say in the South to temper the statement that precedes it, to show it is said out of concern only and never malice. In this case, it might be something like, "She has the taste of a two-bit ho, bless her heart," or "Well, at least they distract you from her hair, bless her heart."

But every dog of a shoe has its day and for this one, Mardi Gras might be it. Definitely a costume party. You can go as the girl who bought the ridiculous shoes. Or are they boots? Or are they socks that escaped from the circus? What ever they are, let's hope they're not breeding.

Designed by a Sadist

You've never been to Eastern Europe, but somehow your shoes seem to speak with an accent thicker than your jet-black eyeliner. "I am ultra hip. I never smile. I have no time for anyone who does not recognize that these shoes were inspired by the works of Nietzsche. If you're seeing me outside, I'm so pale I look invisible. It is irrelevant, you troglodyte, that my shoes nearly draw blood with every step. They are at the height of neo-modern-classic design and, therefore, worthy of my wearing."

Lost in MommyLand

We hear you, and can't miss seeing you. "I'm so cute, even frumpy works for me. My biological clock never ticked, it pounded. My social life is now split between mommy-and-me classes and the swings at the playground. I'm surrounded by one or more munchkins at all times. I've gotten so wrapped up in hunting for 'cute' things for my little centers-of-the-universe, I've completely forgotten I'm a grown woman and I do not need to dress like a character from Romper Room."

Gotta Love the Eighties

"Like, for sure . . ." You found a style you love and aren't letting go. You brilliantly bought thirty-seven pairs before the decade ended and cry at the thought of the day your last pair takes its last valley girl breath.

Your hair is still a homage to metal bands and the new fashions frustrate you because they don't have room to add shoulder pads.

Still Dreaming of Genies

Your bellybutton has long since won its freedom to see the light of day. Whether it should or not. Your ideal living room boasts a circle couch with lots of tufted pillows. You have accounts at three local mystic shops and your psychic is on speed dial.

When someone speaks of flowing sheers, you immediately think clothing, not window treatments. And if you ever get a last minute invite to a costume party, you don't need to add much to your everyday attire to compete for best costume.

Height Challenged, Rejoice

Your "height enhancers" are as subtle as a bad toupee and your insurance carrier would drop you—farther than you might fall—if they ever got a look at these. But you don't care, you're tired of looking everyone in the naval and, in your mind, you're already a six-foot Amazon. Your personality takes up most of the space in a room, which is good, because you need a little chutzpah to pull off tramping around in overgrown platforms.

Mod Gone Mad

These curvaceous little wonders have escaped from the past and have found a déjà vu refuge in your swinging pad. Your furniture is known by the name of its designer and the originals were created before you were born. You never worry about being out of date. You look at your retro world as merely being ahead of the next time designers bring it back in style.

Not Even in Rome

Hello fad girl. What are you doing? Not even on vacation in Greece and from your senses, should you do what the Romans did. Some designer got a good deal on leather strapping and figured someone out there would be gullible enough to spend half an hour strapping herself in. They require tightness akin to a tourniquet, so your legs squeeze out here and there while your feet turn purple.

Yes, that supermodel looked amazing on the runway. So confident and "Wow!" Well, news flash! You don't look as great waiting in line for the bus. And it's not particularly sexy to stop in the middle of the dance floor to retrieve the pile of straps that have fallen down around your ankles. You'll wear them once and then, into the shoe graveyard that is the bottom of your closet they go.

The Curtain is Calling

These are perfectly adorable on those with cherub faces, bows in their ringlet curls, and fewer than double-digit candles on their birthday cakes. They are impressive on those who really meant it when they said, "I'm going to be a ballerina when I grow up."

And on anyone else? They say, "Oh, please pay attention to me. I just found a new wrinkle and desperately need to hear I'm a pretty, pretty princess. And I know you're not laughing at me. You're simply envious of my cuteness."

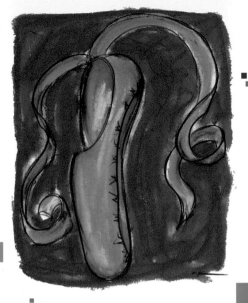

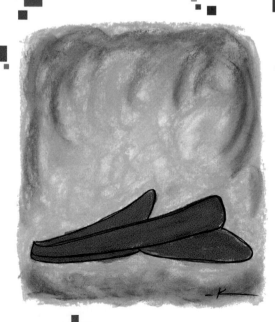

Junk in the Trunk

As you pass by, your fellow shoe aficionados sit perplexed. If life came with those handy little thought bubbles, the looks on their faces would be explained. "What is she thinking?" "Fashion Police, 911!" "Where would you buy those?" "Are they supposed to make her butt look smaller by comparison?" "Please make it stop!"

If you're really, really lucky you might cross paths with a fashion elitist wannabe, who'll insist to her companions in a condescending tone, "Ugly is the latest trend. Haven't you seen the new collections?"

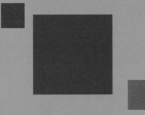

Slipping into Slippers

Cozy, anyone? Before and after every pair we can possibly wear, there are our slippers. A refuge from the stiletto-clad day, they are a tiny bit of heaven that helps us relive the bliss of childhood, a hug dedicated solely to our toes. Slippers are our sappy movie and pint of Rocky Road companions. We can't help but love how they feel, but might prefer they not be seen or heard.

Fuzzy Refuge

Every stiletto girl has a second love. They are soft and squishy—not a hard edge, strap, buckle, or spike in sight. These fuzzies curl up on the couch with you, never scuff a pedicure, and at 5 a.m., when you're still half asleep, they never let your feet feel the chill of your imported marble floor.

You're secretly looking for a man who will treat you as well.

Granny Delights

Sure, bedroom attire may be all the rage right now with lingerie inspired tops as evening wear, but hitting the nightclubs in granny slippers isn't the same thing. Even if it's only a trip to the market, you're still taking the casual thing way too far.

One look at these and the world is expecting curlers and a fuzzy robe. Your foot attire says there is a pile of ironing somewhere in your house, probably in front of the TV, which is permanently tuned to soaps. Your cooking skills consist of dialing for take-out and your longest relationship is with your cats, Mr. Buster and Miss Bimbo.

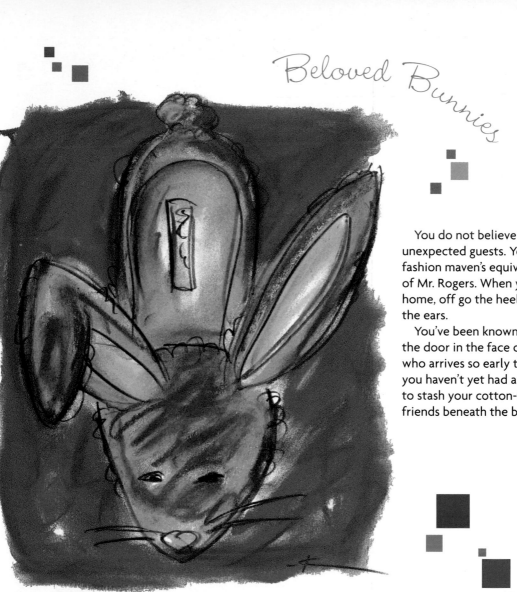

You do not believe in unexpected guests. You're the fashion maven's equivalent of Mr. Rogers. When you get home, off go the heels, on go the ears.

You've been known to slam the door in the face of a date who arrives so early that you haven't yet had a chance to stash your cotton-tailed friends beneath the bed.

Embroider Me a Story

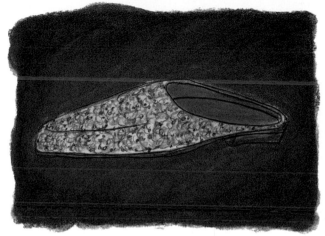

You found them on your latest *fabulous* trip to somewhere *fabulous*. In this *fabulous* little market, you haggled like the locals with this *fabulously* authentic market woman. These gems were hand made, with hand-stitched fabric and hand-carved heels, with leather soles from the family's herd they raise in the mountains above the village. When you wear them, they magically transport you back to the sights and sounds of that *fabulous* place.

Luckily you were able to remove the "Made in Taiwan" tag without leaving a mark. Isn't it *fabulous*?

Big Bird Issues

Every day after school, and we're talking straight through to sophomore year, you sat glued to the TV, waiting in anticipation for the bird of your dreams. You've never told anyone your true love is tall, yellow, and of the feathered variety. As you shuffle to the kitchen for your morning coffee, you flip to PBS, hoping to catch a glimpse. You're sure these fluffy golden blobs would win the big guy over.

It's probably wise to stick to your story that they were a gift from your 6-year-old niece, because the truth should only be shared with your therapist. Preferably soon, very soon.

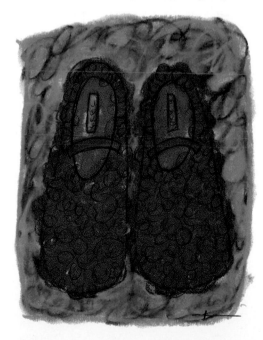

So Much to Say

Most women learn by the age of 18 months that their shoes can separate them from all the other feet, legs, and smiles out there in the world. Once we figured out Cinderella's fairy tale was all about the shoes, we understood our mission: find the loves of our lives and then walk off into the sunset wearing them. But who would have thought our faithful companions would be dishing the dirt on who we really are and telling everyone our secrets?

Now that you've studied Shoe-ology—and hopefully learned a thing or two—maybe you've purged your closet, spent three days and three months' pay buying all new shoes, or taken a vow of solelessness. Just remember that a healthy dose of attitude—good, bad, or bitchy—can translate nearly any shoe into the statement you were going for.